The Case for Conservatism

THREE LECTURES DELIVERED
AT THE UNIVERSITY OF WASHINGTON

By

FRANCIS GRAHAM WILSON

Seattle : University of Washington Press : 1951

FOREWORD

IN terms of contemporary politics, it is reasonably clear that liberalism and conservatism are moderately meaningful terms. But the dichotomy is subject to much confusion when projected against a wider historical background. Are there long time typically liberal and conservative views with respect to any set of grand issues?

To be sure, there *are* liberal and conservative attitudes in the sense of psychological dispositions, and these may be as indelible as W. S. Gilbert suggested in certain memorable lines from *Iolanthe*. This, however, does not guarantee any persistent correspondence with concrete issues. It may, in time, well become a conservative disposition to embrace precisely the point of view once rejected as entirely too "liberal." Nor does it help to define liberalism as synonomous with the Western political tradition, for this scarcely leaves room for a correlative conservative pattern of ideas. Moreover, conservatives may easily retaliate by relating liberalism so narrowly to the "Enlightenment" as to undermine *its* claim to venerable tradition.

Francis Wilson's lectures on conservatism represent a

genuinely philosophical approach to this problem. He has endeavored to generalize upon the content of conservative thought without reducing the result to a mere psychological bent or disposition. I am far from sure that the reader will feel disposed to accept the interpretation of history which Wilson uses to reveal continuity of ideological pattern amidst great ideological changes, but he will find much thoroughly digested history and many highly intriguing insights—which is, after all, precisely what those of us who have known him for many years, including the ten which he spent at the University of Washington, have learned to expect of him.

KENNETH C. COLE
Professor of Political Science
University of Washington

CONTENTS

v

THE CONSERVATIVE SPIRIT IN POLITICS

I

IT is difficult for me to express my pleasure in being again for a few days on the campus of the University of Washington. I did not remember clearly the beauty of the campus, and in this my sight and my mind have been clearly refreshed. Nor could I quite imagine, until I came, the great expansion of the University and the changes that have taken place. But it has required no visit to remind me of the able colleagues and warm friends I have at this University. Perhaps I should speak for a moment in the vein of Henry Adams and suggest another and deeper reason for my appreciation of this University. Henry Adams looked upon his life as a constant process of education, and in retrospect I can see that my life at the University of Washington was an important part of my education. I think I learned a few things when I was here, though what I shall say today must not be considered as evidence of it. Because my stay on this campus is so important a part of the lifelong educational process, this University will always be regarded by me with affection and respect.

I am going to speak to you about the spirit of conservatism in politics. But in so doing I had best clear away some misconceptions related to my subject. As far as I know, there are only a few utopian thinkers who have believed it is possible to have a static society. Social theory in the West has recognized that society is in a continual state of dynamic tension and change, and therefore conservatism, like any other social philosophy, must be in part a theory of change. It must recognize change, advocate it, and resist it, as the case may be. But conservatism as a living political force has not believed that society can be made static by human political art or prudence, nor can one say that the articulate conservatives have advocated such a situation as an ideal. Conservatism is rather, in this respect, a philosophy of social evolution, in which certain lasting values are defended within the framework of the tension of political conflict. And when given values are at stake the conservative can even become a revolutionary, though not to the extent the Marxians assert in their theory of the conservative counterrevolution.

Again, one cannot say that conservatism in politics is a clearcut and fixed program of action or inaction. Conservatism is primarily a spirit animating political behavior, it is a way of life, and it is a manner of judging life. It is this rather than a party platform with a certain number of planks that for the moment, and for the moment only, are regarded as immutable. In this, conservatism is not markedly different from other points of view among the contending ideologies of our time. Who can say with assurance just what a liberal stands for? Liberalism has evolved just as conservatism has, and the liberalism of a hundred years ago has about the same relevance to our day that the conservatism of a century ago might have. There is much outmoded conservatism, just as there is much outmoded socialism. The revolution of yesterday no longer kindles enthusiasm, and it does not evoke a loyalty that will lead men to surrender their lives before its deserted altars. Unlike the revolutionary, however, the conservative might say that we must live with the consequences of past revolutions whatever our feelings may be. As any other philosophy or spirit of politics, conservatism must adapt itself to the necessities of the time, and it must fight its battles on a broken front. As any other social philosophy, it learns to forget the lost cause and the irrelevant tension. It is true, of course, that some conservatives, like some radicals or liberals, never learn anything and never forget what they have failed to learn. But this is not the kind of conservatism that governs our or any other society. The platform of the moment is not the one that governs us tomorrow.

Having suggested that conservatism is a theory of change, and that it is a spirit of politics rather than a fixed program, I should also remind you that I am speaking of articulate and intellectual conservatism. I am not concerned with the inarticulate acceptance of primitive tradition. Intellectual conservatism has at its command the whole range of philosophy and science that the centuries of Western civilization have provided. The conservatism of our society is not an unexpressed sentiment or mere emotion of resignation to things as they are, nor is it so anywhere in the West. I am sure that many liberals would like to treat the conservatism of public opinion and the political leadership of Europe and America as a mere primitive survival; but they know, as well as anyone else, that such an argument is simply a series of epithets that has no rational meaning. Intellectual conservatism is, therefore, a continuous evaluation of the past, the present, and the future. It assumes that there are some primary values that change little, if at all, and that there are secondary levels of judgment and action that change almost from day to day. The program of any conservative group becomes, therefore, a secondary element, and primary intellectual conservatism is used as a standard of value to judge the imperfections of actual political controversy.

II

With these ideas in mind, let us inquire now into the origin of conservatism as a conscious political movement in the modern world. I think it can be said that the shock of the French Revolution and the story of the uninspiring consequences flowing from that revolution gave rise to conservatism as we know it today. As the generous and humane sentiments of the early leaders of that movement gave place to more stubborn and revolutionary figures, as constitutionalism gave place to terror, and as the terror gave place to dictatorship and a French dream of world conquest, it was natural that those who wished to escape the net of conquest and subjugation should consider the grounds of their defense. Those of you who know something of the history of political ideas need not be told that every turn in intellectual history is as bitterly and persistently contested as any issue of contemporary politics.

When the French Revolution came, each articulate thinker had to take a stand, just as none today can be indifferent to the Russian Revolution and its consequences. As French liberal ideas began to be heard in England, like a distant roll of thunder giving warning of the approaching storm, Englishmen had to ask themselves whether they had anything that was worth saving. It was Edmund Burke who, in his *Reflections on the Revolution in France,* declared roundly that English society had some virtues that were worthy of preservation. Burke's writings are the doctrinal source of modern conservatism. Historical rationalism, as a response to the abstract rationalism of science, as exemplified in Descartes and others, had already made its appearance in the writings of Vico, Montesquieu, and others, but its intimate political relevance to the time was not seen until the implications of the French Revolution began to appear. Burke was trying to say, I think, that while we must live with history, while we cannot escape its impact upon us, we can also live there with enthusiasm and with loyalty to the historical community of which we are a part. His challenge became known throughout Europe, and the European, living under the blows of the doctrinaires and the dictatorship of the French Revolution, discovered the possibility of the good life in a moving, changing, and evolving historical context.

It is said that Chateaubriand originated the term "conservative" in the year 1818. It was only a few years before it began to be generally used in the controversies of European politics. In 1830 the term was popularized among English-men by a writer in the *Quarterly Review*. At about the same time this descriptive label came into pretty general use in Latin-American politics, and it was not long before parties bearing the name began to make their entrance on the political stage. Conservative parties, so named, were organized in England in 1835, in Germany and France in 1848, and in Spain in 1875, for example. But it can hardly be said that the realities of the conservative position appeared only with parties given this name. It is likewise true that the term "conservative" has never been a very popular and generally used identification. As a spirit in politics, conservatism has fared better under other names, names that have been specifically in accordance with national symbolism.

I have observed that both the liberalism and conservatism of a century ago have changed profoundly in the course of modern history. The institutions that represented continuity in political loyalty and political experience in the years immediately after the French Revolution no longer perform the same role. Burke defended with vigor the English monarchy as it had been constitutionalized by the Revolution of 1688. To him the events of the Glorious Revolution were not a break in British history, for they were, rather, the confirmation of liberty under law that the years of revolution and disturbance during the seventeenth century had endangered. The Whig revolution was a revolution by conservatives in the interest of the preservation of the conditions under which the rights of Englishmen might be respected. The defense of the British Constitution became in the eighteenth century a battle cry of both reformers and opponents of reform, and after the French Revolution the conservative mind throughout Europe was influenced by the argument of Montesquieu, that the British Constitution alone had devoted itself to the preservation of liberty. Thus in continental conservatism during the nineteenth century there was something of the same flavor that had animated the framers of our own constitutional system. It was the ideal of balance, of mixture in the Constitution, so that, as John Adams had argued, no one interest or group might run away with the state. It was, indeed, a continuation of the Aristotelian argument that a good society is balanced between the extremes of rich and poor and between the extremes of democratic and oligarchical techniques of government.

The defense of constitutional balance is no more outmoded than ever—that is, restraint in government is a political virtue. However, the use made of the doctrine on the Continent was often unperceptive, no matter how much it might be influenced by the ideal of the British system, with its monarchy and its emergent parliamentary system. But such an unperceptive conservatism served the purpose of showing that a reaction to legitimism would be no more solidly constructed than the empire of Napoleon. The defense of monarchy in the British Commonwealth is still a conservative symbol, hardly attacked indeed by the socialists who now govern that society. But on the Continent the battle still rages between those who, in France, for example, would like a strong executive, such as the President of the United States, and those who wish to have power completely concentrated in the hands of a parliament. Legitimism no longer can be associated with hereditary succession to the executive power in Europe, but at no time in Western history has the issue of what is a legitimate government been of more importance. Then, as now, constitutionalism is a defense against the hysteria and the extremism of power-hungry minorities, whose answer to criticism is the denial of human liberty and a system of forced labor or state slavery.

Burke's system was a defense of the national tradition, and of the nation-state as the context of the good life. The defense of the nation is surely an inevitable and rational answer to the madness of the conqueror. Nineteenth-century conservatism was clearly nationalistic, but it had no monopoly on this symbol of community life. And the issue might be today whether the abuse of nationalism comes more from those who deny the national rights of states or from those who defend them and who show some respect for the principle of national self-determination. The *Risorgimento* has been regarded by Italians as a revolution by conservatives on behalf of national rights, but until 1929 one of the profound weaknesses of Italian conservatism was its opposition to the national religious tradition of the Italian people. And the Spanish conservatives could see in the defense of the national tradition a means of resisting the intervention in Spanish affairs conducted by those who in the name of legitimacy were using in reality the techniques of Napoleon.

But let us be clear on this point. The early nineteenth-century expression of conservatism in Europe has little relevance to the problems that we face today. On the fringes of the extreme right there are small groups who may still think in terms of the legitimacy of a hundred years ago, and they may be exhibited for social purposes on occasion; but as effective conservatives and as representative conservatives, they have long since passed from the theatre of active politics. From the pen of the conservative today, like that of Winston Churchill, comes a plea for the consent of the governed in the light of the tradition of the people. Legitimacy is a defense of free government, government by consent, and the acceptance of change within the framework of the tradition of community life.

Political struggle in Great Britain has been focused between the Conservatives or Tories against the Whigs; later between the Conservatives and the Liberals; and still later between the inevitably resurgent conservatism and the newer Labor party. In this change of positions, the Liberal has found that his emergent position is with the conservative against the newer issue and the deeper challenge to the social order. Liberalism has thus demonstrated historically its lack of content, and it has been left to the new revolutionaries of our day to take it up and to identify themselves with the angels by using it.

In the United States our political parties have been, on primary matters, essentially conservative, and the split between them, as less or more conservative, has generally been on secondary matters of program. Before the Confederate War, for example, Southern agrarians looked on the South as the conservative balance wheel of the Union, for they believed that the evils of industrialism would destroy the

American tradition. But since 1865 conservatism in the
United States has been committed to the preservation of
the Union, to the maintenance of constitutional tradition,
and to the development of an industrial and commercial
society. Thus the English liberals and conservatives have
had much in common with American conservatism. But
when contemporary liberalism supports revolutionary materialism and denies the moral and Christian interpretation
of human nature, it is clearly opposed to the American conservative tradition. In the European conservative mind, the
landed interest has included, by definition, the landlord, the
tenant, and the worker, and it has believed in the defense
of this interest even under modern industrial conditions.
For us, such terminology is remote from the daily language,
but in so far as we have believed that the interests of land-
lords can be reconciled with those of tenants, our theory of
agricultural tenure has not been different in essentials from
the European system.

The most significant change in the uncertain flux of
division between the conservative and the revolutionary
spirits of politics has come about by the gradual emergence
of Marxism as a powerful political philosophy. If one con-
siders the battle between the conservative spirit and its
liberal opponents in our daily politics, we can still recognize
a great, if undefined, community of ideas behind both. Here
the struggle is perhaps between what might be called conservatism and liberalism. But if we consider international
questions, the conflict is changed markedly. For here the
struggle is between those who see some value in the continuity of Western philosophy and institutions, and those

who support the newer revolutionary conception of society, and, I might add, whatever tyranny is bred by that philosophy in its political practice. The conflict here then is between conservatism and revolutionism.

Marxism has changed profoundly the conservative opposition to revolution. For dialectical materialism has denied the essential intellectual positions of Western conservatism as well as those of Western liberalism. Marxism has demanded a revolution that would overthrow private property in capital, modern competitive enterprise, and Christian moral philosophy. Moreover, Marxism has shown no respect for the idea of balance or restraint in either government or in individuals; it has seen no point in any limitation on governmental power, or in the idea of the mixed constitution of which our own system has been no pale reflection. The millenial social ends that Marxism has formulated are to be attained, as in the current areas of Slavic control, by whatever political power is necessary. Socialism, as the validation of economic revolution, has come to be, during the last few generations, the chief critic of conservatism. Doctrinally, conservatives have tended to state their position as a defense of a free-market economy, but in fact it resembles more that of a moderate and mixed system of economic organization. In opposition to the perfectionism of socialism, conservatism has rejected the unlimited power of the state in establishing a planned or proletarian system. On specific issues, it may well happen that conservatives and revolutionists will be found on the same side of the fence; but this is a secondary matter, for the alliance can in no sense be permanent, and the grounds for taking a common posi-

in the conservatism of Burke, believed that the good life must be sought in the context of time and social evolution. This idea has been different from the more ancient use of history. Machiavelli, for example, believed, like the ancients, that history taught by example, often the isolated example offered by the life of a political leader, as in Plutarch's *Lives*. The statesman, for Machiavelli, might learn his statecraft by looking at minute segments of the past, and he might apply these rather easily learned lessons to any particular time and place. History was a pattern in that individual lives demonstrated repetitiously the art of rulership. In other words, there was no specific rationalism and no organic continuity in history. There was, instead, example, and the lesson it might teach. Beginning with the early eighteenth century, Vico suggested there was a pattern of social evolution in history and that one must learn from history over a much longer span than had been thought useful before. Burke is the heir of Vico, just as he is the heir of Montesquieu, and just as Hegel is the heir of all of them. But the lesson that Burke and Hegel taught was that while there was a pattern in history, each nation had to learn its own lesson from its own national tradition.

The application of such ideas to the immediate problem of government, to the construction of a legitimate and workable regime, is, I think, fairly obvious. It is a response to the unhistorical liberalism of the seventeenth century, whether in science or motivated by religious conflict. It is a response to the new creeds of utilitarian politics and to a psychology that assumed each man started the race with a blank mind. It was a response, more particularly, to the theorists of the French Revolution who held that clear-headed people might sit down in a room and construct with the pen a new society in which all the ancient frustrations of men would be forgotten. Tom Paine today is a vigorous and interesting thinker, but I believe that most of us would rather have Edmund Burke in a new constitutional convention.

Paine, the doctrinaire, was a destroyer of the old, both here and in France, but when it came to the establishment of an orderly and lasting government, this greatest of all propagandist geniuses faded rapidly from the picture. True, in a time of upheaval the destroying breath of liberal anger may serve the cause of the revolution, but when the day arrives for restoring an order under which men can do their daily work, the lessons of history, as shown in the evolution of the national community, have also their place.

From another point of view, we might ask whether the defense of the British Constitution during the years after the French Revolution served a worthy purpose. The fact that the continuity of British institutions was preserved in a time of trouble has, in the present hour, given encouragement that democracy may still flourish on the Continent of Europe, and that the night of a totalitarian age is not an inevitability. From the continuity of British institutions both democracy, in its parliamentary form, and industrialism have been offered to the world. On the Continent, the hope is not that our institutions of government will be copied, but that the ancient parliamentary system, already copied once during the nineteenth century, may be copied again, and perhaps this time be made to work with more effectiveness. Such a hope is clear in the program for European recovery, and it is clear in our defense of the free election against the drive of Slavic totalitarianism. As Europeans have admired the British system since the end of the seventeenth century, so today one assurance of recovery, both politically and economically, emerges from the fact of British historical evolution, rather than doctrinaire reform. We take as our hope one part of the pattern of history, not the isolated example, but the long example, the example that is to be found in the national experience of the British, and the suggestion that the national traditions of Europe can be the basis of orderly life.

Let us consider, second, the issue of human nature. With the Enlightenment in the eighteenth century, the idea came to be held strongly that man is by nature perfectible, and that he is corrupted or irrational only because of the force of institutions. In contrast, the historical position has been that man is a child of God, that he is sinful or corrupted, but that he is also rational and capable of living up to the standards of reason, provided he is taught to do so, and provided, in Christian thought, that he is aided by grace. It is obvious that to assume institutions are bad, and man is bad because he is a product of them, opened wide the way to proposals for reform and for the fundamental alteration of society. The conservative, in response, has generally believed that institutions are reflective of human nature, but the process of improving men is slow, and the concept of evolution has been used to buttress the principle of limited reform and slow progress toward a millenial age. While revolutionary philosophy, from the French Revolution on, has sustained the idea of revolt against institutions, the conservative mind, following the lead of Burke, has believed that such revolt is rather against man because it destroys the context in which man has made progress. The revolutionist wants to make all his money at once, while the conservative is often content to save his pennies, in the hope that the bank will be good at some future but not unpredictable time. The adjustment of the conservative mind to popular sovereignty can thus be reconciled with principle, since the conservative would, like Woodrow Wilson, assume that democracy is the product of growth and habit, and that men must be worthy of freedom before it can be successfully thrust upon them.

But if we look at the contemporary scene, it is clear that these ideas have considerable import in our effort to recover from the destructiveness of more than thirty years of war and revolution. The conservative attitude suggests the slow and painful stages through which we hope we shall move toward the restoration of a world that has at least some resemblance to the world of the nineteenth century. Utopia will not come, because man is not a being suited for a political utopia. Since war and revolution have destroyed socially necessary institutions, these must be rebuilt on the basis of what will work. Recovery in Europe is restoration; it means connecting again the links with the past, the healing of the wounds in national tradition, and the expansion through society again of the idea of security and the rule of law. When restoration of the elemental principles of order, political and economic, has been achieved, it will be time enough to consider what reforms will be workable. In any case, each society must be left to work out much of its unhappy destiny in this process of restoration. Today, when we defend free elections and the right of peoples to have an orderly democracy, undisturbed by the revolutionary utopian, we are asserting the necessity of continuity and order as the basis of European civilization. But it is being done in an atmosphere of compromise where possible, and with a recognition that ends should not be set too high in the short span of time.

One might add, I think, that the criticism of doctrinaire liberalism rests heavily on the principle that human nature, as an observable and historical fact, does not support the ideas of the liberal system. And it should be noted that leaders, in whatever crusade we may consider, are easily persuaded that men must be forced to be free, to use Rousseau's idea, when they do not seem capable of proceeding on the same path of unanimity as those who have political power in their grasp. The conservative may say, indeed, that totalitarian systems are likely to be the logical consequence of assuming that men are better than their institutions, for then any obstruction to progress is clearly a matter of either ignorance or of hypocrisy.

In the third place, the conservative mind has insisted on the existence of some kind of moral order as the criterion of life and the trusteeship of power. This moral order is one of the oldest products of Western society, for it begins in the Greek distinction between nature and convention; it flowers in the concept of natural law in Roman civil law and in Christian philosophy, and, while the term "natural law" is used today for the most part among Catholic thinkers, the principle is expressed in Protestant thought by the idea of a moral order, and in Jewish thinking by the notion of divine justice. It was re-expressed at Nürnberg when we accused the Nazi leaders of having committed crimes against humanity. It arises again, and always again, when we face the intolerable abuses of tyranny, or when men would preserve against the encroachments of society some fragments of their spiritual freedom. While the Roman civil law said, finally, that the will of the prince has the force of law, that legal system carried forward also the idea of the *ius naturale,* just as Christianity has always insisted on the fact that man is a child of God and owes to him some form of obedience. The reason of God must, to the Christian, summarize the moral order of the world.

Now the conservative mind will say, I think, that the moral order is, finally, the basis on which any preservation of the benefits of a historically continuous civilization must be realized. True, the "realistic" conservatives are little concerned, if at all, with any moral ideals or ultimate goals; all that is necessary is that the great agencies of control, the army, the bureaucracy, the law, the police, and even the churches, perform their appropriate roles in the government of man. The empire they build is mechanical, and the external proletariat, as Toynbee might say, can easily overthrow their system when it has come toward its end. These conservatives are Machiavellian in spirit; they have been the great defenders of reason of state and exceptional or dictatorial powers being vested in government. But such a conservatism is a disease and it occurs in a time of spiritual and moral flatness. In contrast, the long-run conservative tradition has believed that government must represent the total body of social interests; it has drawn its standards from the moral tradition of the West; and it has been of the opinion that the sacred rights of man must be defended by government, not through doctrinaire pronouncements but in the tradition of theistic respect for the individual. It is this kind of conservatism that has given rise to creative and not parasitic but dominant minorities. It is the kind of conservatism that wrote the Constitution of the United States, and it is the kind of conservatism that has enabled the British system to change and to persist through many and startling phases of history.

But perhaps more important than all of this, the conservative defense of the moral order, the moral order that has emerged from Jewish, Roman, and Christian tradition, is the only answer we have today to the corrosive doctrine of the class struggle. For the principle of a moral order assumes that all men participate in it, or can if they will, and it assumes the community of moral responsibility is greater than the economic and divisive material differences that enable one to preach the class struggle. Ideas and a common spirit can unite a people, but material interests most surely divide. And if we are spiritual eunuchs it is easy for us to kill each other in a struggle for unlimited power and for the wealth that the common efforts of all may have produced in any society.

Now, in the fourth place, let us consider briefly the idea of limited, restrained, or balanced government. If I may say that the idea of inevitable class struggle is the most terrible illusion of our time, another closely related to it, and one that is almost as destructive to civilized order and social progress, is the belief that power must be unlimited, that it must be concentrated in the hands of a single segment of a total population, and that any political devices that even delay the exercise of this power are the works of reaction. Let me remind you that democracy rests on a spirit of consensus in society; it rests on the belief that the interests of all can be reflected in the labor of administration and in the determination of public policy; it rests, indeed, on the idea that all of the community must be served with justice, rather than that some sections of society must be suppressed and finally destroyed with death or slavery.

Our democracy—indeed, any democracy that has long survived—has believed that government is responsible to the community, but that responsibility must be exercised with restraint and moderation, under the rule of law. This, I think, is the meaning of constitutionalism in the West, as it has emerged from the ancient world, through the Middle Ages, and in the modern period. The democrat has said that a revolution is unjustified so long as the preconditions of majority rule are observed. These preconditions of majority rule have been stated in the bill of rights, primarily the right to life, liberty, and property. To believe that democracy means the exercise of power by unrestricted majorities, controlling and destroying the rule of law, is to deny the foundations of democracy from the very beginning. Democracy has meant, indeed, that when the rights of the individual are restricted it must be done through the rule of law, and that any deprivation of rights carries only the immediate consequences of that restriction. It has meant, as Locke said, that legislatures as well as majorities are under the law of nature.

But we should ask, I think, more specifically how government has been limited in the now emergent theory of Western conservatism. I have suggested that a bill of rights, whose interpretation is eventually within the power of the courts of law, is one of the first lines of defense in protecting limitation on government. But in addition to the idea of a written constitution that states the rules of the game for a political society, there are other devices. These devices fall under the heading of the mixed constitution, the constitution that is balanced between different social groups, regions or interests, with the result that political decision is essentially a compromise between different social groups, regions, or interests. Our own Constitution clearly reflects this idea, so ably stated by Montesquieu, Blackstone, and DeLolme in the eighteenth century. For a division in the legislative branch, as in the United States, represents different regions; it gives different social groups differing points of focus, and it gives various social interests more than one place to offer pressure on the course of public decision. Along with this principle of balance, we have the separation of powers which acts as a system of self-protection and checking between the formally established branches of the government. I believe it can be argued that Montesquieu, for example, was primarily concerned with the mixed constitution and only secondarily with the separation of powers. But whatever may have been his chief interest, he was determined that political liberty should be preserved. And such a preservation of liberty must come at least in part through the moderation of the impact of government on the individual.

The revolutionary mind of our generation has grown sharply impatient of any limitations on government. The Continental theory of majority rule suggests that the minority has no real rights against the existing majority, and that civil liberty is in reality a grant of that majorty. Likewise, the contemporary revolutionary, as in France recently, has opposed the strengthening of the executive and any political devices that might slow down the process of legislation. One might add that in Britain, even though the majority is technically free, the success of the system has depended on the survival of a tradition of the rule of gentlemen who clearly observe the rules of the game.

Finally, the conservative mind has defended the institution of private property. The great legal systems of the West, the Roman civil law, and the English common law, stand side by side on this question, and, as I have said, the law of property is antecedent to the modern changes in the economic system, or to the rise of capitalism. To defend the system of private property we must turn to the moral tradition of the West, to the principles of justice that have surely evolved and maintained themselves through many centuries. But the belief in property arises, I think, from a belief in the family as the primary social unit, and property in a functional sense has been connected with the survival of the family group. If one believes in the Christian principle of the family, one can easily believe that property is a natural adjunct to the moral function of the family. While the ideas of social Christianity in the last two generations have attacked certain abuses and certain forms of property, it can hardly be said that Protestantism has attacked property, and clearly the Catholic Encyclicals have defended it function- ally as a means of preserving the independence and the standard of living of the family. I do not think one needs to say that the defense of property means that we must defend a theoretical system of laissez-faire, that, in fact, has never existed except in the mind of liberal protest. Laissez- faire is as millenarian a doctrine as the theories of Marxian socialism. A correction of the abuses of industrialism is a problem different from the moral defense of property, and it may be argued that property can be preserved only by reforms in the centralized, urban-industrial complex of modern society.

IV

Let us now attempt to define and summarize what has been said. Conservatism as a political attitude strives to balance stability and order against doctrinaire progress and careless reform. The conservative spirit bases a belief in moderation in reform on two primary points. It believes that human nature is a combination of reason and unselfishness and of irrational and recalcitrant behavior. But it also believes that because men make history and social institu- tions, experience can be a guide to what will be lasting and effective change. Yet the experience that any social group may use is embodied largely in tradition, though any national tradition is also in part universal, or for us it is at least as comprehensive as Western civilization. Intellectual conservatism, as contrasted with primitive traditionalism, believes in the permanence of social principles as historical guides to order and progress. The belief in the religious and moral nature of man and the attendant social code, the defense of property, the insistence on limited political authority, the belief in liberty and individual autonomy, the security of the nation, the maintenance of the middle class, opposition to revolution, and the value of public order are primary, historical conservative ideas. But conservative principle or primary conservatism must be distinguished from changing and temporary secondary conservative programs. For experience, as contained in religion and moral standards, in scientific and technological advance, and in the arts, is of greater durability than political policies urged to meet particular social situations.

The conservative spirit would hold, I believe, that democracy is a direct outgrowth of its principles; it cannot believe that democracy is possible outside of experience preserved in legal institutions and in historic constitutionalism. The socialist revolutionary interprets these principles as a covering for the maneuvers of the capitalist ruling class. The specific and immediate form of the conflict has been the program of the Left, whether revolutionary or otherwise, for the socialization of the economy in the interest of the general welfare. The conservative spirit in politics has opposed this demand by supporting political freedom and regulated competition.

MUST THE RIGHT GO LEFT?*

IN the year 1889 Woodrow Wilson reviewed at length the recently published *American Commonwealth* by James Viscount Bryce. That work was the greatest study of American institutions since the publication in 1835 of Alexis de Tocqueville's *Democracy in America.* Woodrow Wilson thus took the opportunity to write an essay, deeply evaluative in tone, of the American system. But it was an essay that was also prophetic, and it is one of those prophetic utterances that I wish now to call to your attention. For Woodrow Wilson said, perhaps in the spirit of Burke from whom he had drawn so much, "America is now sauntering through her resources and through the mazes of her politics with easy nonchalance; but presently there will come a time when she will be surprised to find herself grown old,—a country crowded, strained, perplexed,—when she will be obliged to fall back upon her conservatism, obliged to pull herself together, adopt a new regimen of life, husband her resources, concentrate her strength, steady her methods,

---

* Part of this lecture is taken from an article, "The Contemporary Right," *The Western Political Quarterly,* Vol. 1 (September, 1948), pp. 287-294. It is used with the consent of the editor.

sober her views, restrict her vagaries, trust her best, not her average members. That will be the time of change."

Now what I wish to ask you this evening is whether that time, prophesied by Woodrow Wilson, has arrived. May I say that I think it has? But may I suggest also that in a brief paragraph he has offered the firm outlines of the conservative creed for our time. I think it may be argued that in many ways our present-day policies are experimental approaches to a fundamental readjustment of American life to the new conditions of mid-twentieth-century crisis. As with all experiments, much will be tried that is of little value, but much will remain as the foundation for the future. It will remain, I think, just in proportion as it is an intellectual application of the primary conservatism of the West, and just in proportion as it is an application, under new conditions, of the basic ideas on which our national tradition has been constructed.

The experiments of which I speak are being tried on the two broad and natural fronts of political action. We are determined to preserve a continuity in our economic and political system at home, but we are also forced to many new positions, many restatements of foreign policy, in our relations with the rest of the world. Few responsible political leaders will say they wish to destroy private property, the private accumulation of capital, or hinder the onward movement of technology. Even the mystic Henry Agard Wallace liked to think of himself as the savior of our system of economic enterprise. The conflict centers on a narrow focus, for it concerns what policies will best enable our historic and traditional system to serve the humanitarian ideals of the nation. As we struggle to preserve the system of free enterprise, we also labor to make our republican and democratic ideals suitable for life in the midst of this century of war and revolution. Again the conflict is closely focused and sharp. In foreign policy, we begin slowly to realize that, since the attack on Pearl Harbor and the introduction of the atomic bomb, any argument for an old-style isolation is about as remote from the immediate facts of life as the debate on chattel slavery before the Confederate War, or whether the Jeffersonian criticism of the Hamiltonian industrial system should in this day be taken seriously.

We see as through a darkened glass, for we do not really know what we ought to do, whether to preserve the political and economic system or to sustain ourselves against a hostile, Slavic coalition, that daily distorts the reality of our lives in its propaganda, and defames our name as a defender of freedom in its judicial and political procedures. But we are trying, we are experimenting, and there is energy in our determination to see it through. For as President Roosevelt said in his Third Inaugural Address, we as a nation have a mind, a body, and a future. But it is the future that requires the most sacred guarding in the present crisis of American society.

II

I feel that some discussion of present-day American political parties should be presented before we go any further. As you are aware, it is commonly said that the Republican party is the party of conservatism while the Democratic party is the party of liberalism. By this I suppose we mean that the Democratic party has, in some senses, a more liberal tradition in its distinguished history than does the Republican party. I have heard this argument made, for example, by former Governor Arnall of Georgia, but it is not a proposition that can be taken without some examination. Can it be denied that opposition to the extension of slavery to the territories, the political force that, in measure, gave rise to the Republican party, was not humanitarian and liberal, as these words are often used? Can it be denied that the progressive movement has been shared by both parties, and that in fact there are some rather stubborn people in both parties? One must say, I think, that Southern Democrats are far more attached to their tradition than some Middle Western Republicans, such as those who follow Colonel McCormick and his Chicago *Tribune*. And, if one turns to the historic statements that are used to show the traditional liberalism of Democrats, one must also remember that Democrats have, historically, stood for states' rights and against the expansion of federal functions proposed in the name of humanitarian impulse.

I happened to be in Washington just at the time Jefferson Memorial was opened to the public. Around the inside of that monument are highly selected quotations from the man who is supposed to be the first father of the Democratic party. But those quotations are very carefully chosen and there is nothing in them to reflect Jefferson's opposition to frenzied federal finance, to control by the federal judiciary of the state courts, his opposition to more than two presidential terms, or his dislike of increased federal functions. Jefferson talked on every side of many questions during his long life, but during his last years he became very intimate with John Adams, who certainly is supposed to reflect the ideas of the conservative Federalists. In the letters that passed between Jefferson and John Adams there are moments when they tried to decide just how they had differed when they were in public office. But neither Adams nor Jefferson made a very convincing case that they had differed in principle at all.

What I wish to suggest by these observations is that it is easy to confuse principles with the conflicts of personalities as they struggle for public office. The truth is, I believe, that both the Democratic and Republican parties are, by tradition and political behavior, essentially conservative parties. It can be said that at certain times one or the other of them may be more or less conservative than at other times, but in measure most of the American people believe in their political system. They are hostile to both the great and the small attack upon it. In the South the people vote Democratic, and, as a rule, outside the great cities of the North and West Coast, people vote Republican. Liberalism is primarily a big-city movement, and it is only there that one will find groups devoted to the overthrow of the American system. It arises in part, I think, from the inevitable insecurity, frustration, and helplessness that many people who make up the population of the great cities are almost certain to feel, simply from the conditions of their lives.

Governor Dewey recently argued that there are deep splits in the Republican party, but it is quite easy to argue that the split in the Democratic party is even more profound. Both parties will get together at election time in order to elect a president, but after the election the division in Congress represents the real sentiments and the splits in the parties, for in Congress, I would argue, we come closer than at election time to the deeply grounded public opinion of the American people. A Democratic president cannot be elected unless he gets a large big-city vote, and the only way this vote can be gathered to the Democratic fold is by promising to relieve the frustration that thousands of city inhabitants feel. But to get the big-city vote he must forget about the Southern Democrats, and he must assume that, come what may, they will vote Democratic. Then when Congress meets he is clearly unable to carry out his promises, since the Southern Democrats will not vote for a program that has little relation to their political tradition and their system of social values. May I say that I see little chance of ending this situation, and that recent events point to an even deeper and more permanent split in the Democratic party? Only so long as the Southerners vote solidly Democratic on election day can the Democrats, under present conditions, elect a president of the United States.

What conclusion can one draw from this argument? It is clear that conservative thought in the United States is divided between the two major parties, and one may either say that both parties are conservative or that there is no conservative political party in the United States. This split in the ranks of the conservatives makes it necessary for a president to be, in words, more liberal than the rank and file of the people, because it is necessary to get the vote of the large cities in the Democratic column in order to elect a Democrat as president. If the conservative forces of the

happy about the present condition of party life in the United States. The liberal knows in his heart that he cannot win, and the conservative has the moral certainty that, short of a great internal crisis, he cannot lose. But we do not behave that way at election time; I am afraid that we do a lot of pretending from the first of September to election day in an election year. Would it not be better to have a clearer and more effective system of party responsibility? Most of us are committed to the idea of responsible two-party government, a system in which parties have a program that is submitted to the voters on election day, and for which responsibility is assumed for carrying it out through legislative and executive policies. How can we get party responsibility? If my assumption is correct that Congress represents more surely than election alignment the streams of public opinion, then if the alignments in Congress were before the voters on election day there would be more of a sense of choice in the mind of the voter when he is in the secrecy of the voting booth. But that does not occur, because the only way a party can elect a president is through the campaign fiction of party unity. We are caught here in a contradiction between the conservative principles of a majority of the people and the structure of the government that requires unity before a majority can be obtained in the electoral college. On the other hand, if a new alignment of parties should clearly divide the conservative sheep from the radical goats, political conflict would become savage, there would be less compromise between groups, and majorities would become less charitable to minorities.

But I think some of you must be asking: If we assume

that the Republican party is more, or slightly more, conservative, than the Democratic party, does it have any future in American politics? In other words, can the Republicans ever elect another president of the United States? The test, of course, is, in the long run, the urban vote. One might argue that the price of corn had a lot to do with the last election. It might be recalled that no administration has been thrown out of office while the farmer was getting good prices for his crops. One might also note that the Republican vote in a number of urban areas increased in proportion to the Democratic vote, in spite of the Taft-Hartley law. If the Democrats should split effectively between the Dixiecrats and the Northern wing of the party, it is likely that the Republicans would have a chance.

But the problem for the Republicans, who have not taken the lead in proposing legislation for the city population—what we generally call social legislation—is to get or to split the urban vote. How can the Republican party, as the more conservative party, regain its lost hold on the urban voter? It might wait in the hope that the voter, by a swing away from the left, will come back to the Grand Old Party. It might try to imitate the programs of the Democrats, and thus make promises that inevitably the Congress will not fulfill. It might try, as the British Conservatives have done, to formulate a program of its own that offers some hope of increased security for the masses of the people and the avoidance of economic crisis. Such a program, like the Conservative British Industrial Charter, might suggest that there is a reasoned defense of moderate reform that will be persuasive to the people. Since we believe in a two-party system,

I doubt that the Republican party will die in the near future, but I also suspect that many experiments will be tried. Some Middle Western Republicans will want to wait until the voters return; some Eastern Republicans will no doubt, as in the recent past, imitate the Democratic program; and I suspect that on the Pacific Coast, because of the progressive tradition, Republicans will experiment with progressive programs that attempt to give the people some of the things they want.

But I should like to suggest that yesterday's liberal program often becomes uninspiring in the light of today's problems. Liberals have a tendency to slow down, just as any other political group. As liberalism tends to disintegrate, conservatism tends to come to life again. And it is to this problem that we should now turn, in a more general investigation, of the contemporary problem of the conservative mind. Yet I think I should suggest that it is in the field of foreign policy that competing and conflicting ideas are most clearly expressed. In the last election the general agreement of the two major parties, with disagreements in detail, is a case in point, as well as the tendency of the leftwing groups, like the Progressive party under the leadership of Henry Agard Wallace, to be most critical of the national foreign policy.

III

Students of politics have long observed the so-called "law of the pendulum" in politics. This proposition says that there is a secular swing in public appreciation, especially in democracies, between the conservative and liberal spirits of politics. We have here another way of stating the continuous disintegration and reintegration of the force of political symbols. Movements are seldom static in their persuasive force. Liberals like to point to the disintegration of conservative thought, demonstrated by the more trivial of political changes, while conservatives are convinced, in general, of the law of the disintegration of liberalism. Such a conservative position arises from a study of the disappearance of idealism in a movement as it comes closer to the inner circle of power. As T. V. Smith has argued, the greater the element of compromise, that is, effectiveness, in political decision the less becomes the element of ideality. "Quantity and quality of ideality for action are incompatible and so vary inversely," he has declared.

Now the appeal of the liberal is, according to conservative thought, his support of the ideal solution, or the absolutely just situation. But as the liberal comes close to power, the necessities of decision constantly force him away from the lofty nature of his principle. Thus, inevitably as liberalism and revolutionism approach effective organization, its *élan vital* tends to be dissipated in the practicalities of day-to-day politics. Conservatism is, in this theory, never dead, but its vitality tends to be coincident with the operation of the law of the disintegration of liberalism.

On the other hand, as conservative vitality emerges from liberal disintegration there must logically be a period when, as both types of movement are in transition, their ideality and their appeal to the aspirations of men stand in balance, just as their adjustments to the facts of political life stand in adjustment or balance. It would seem that it is at this point that the greatest migration of techniques takes place, and the political devices of one movement may become in measure the devices of the other. The conservatism of transition, in contrast to its historical statements of policy, balances the liberalism of disintegration. The perennial rebirth of conservation becomes apparent as liberalism disintegrates through the falsification of its own revolution.

IV

In a day of transition, such as the present clearly is, both liberalism and conservatism become singularly dynamic, but this mutual dynamism is, no doubt, a product of balanced ideological tension, as well as the external forces of political chaos. The chaos of our day is a reflection of the failure of the consolidated liberalism of another era to reach its goal in the immediate present. In the nature of the case, since liberal and revolutionary idealism is immoderate in its claims, it falls further short of its goal than conservatism. The liberal and the revolutionary mind has cultivated the illusion that the reverse is the case, for they have placed much of their hope of future success in the complete and dismal failure of conservatism in power.

During the last century and a half, since the rise of both conscious liberalism and conservatism, liberalism has been constantly shocked by the survival, the rebirth, the reacquisition of power by the conservative spirit. One of the political advantages of the conservative spirit has been, indeed, the feeling of liberalism that its victory is inevitable and that conservatism, whatever its particular evolutionary theory, is fatally weak and on the verge of falling into dust.

I think liberals as well as conservatives may profit from a study of their lost causes. Possibly, there are no more instructive episodes in this respect than the changing justifications of achievement in the Soviet Union, the liquidation of the Leninist conception of the ideal, the perennial failure of socialism in western Europe to attain power before 1914, and the eternal unwillingness of liberal regimes to admit that now the social system of which they dreamed has been attained. British socialism, perhaps, can never say that socialism as it was preached in the past has now been attained.

The constant rebirth of conservatism shows it to be on somewhat firmer ground. In the first place, its ideals are stated in more moderate terms, and their realization is more clearly perceived to be in an evolutionary context that only long national experience may reveal. In the second place, the ideals that continually are reborn in the conservative spirit are stated in the light of political realities. The conservative, in his nature, can never promise as much as the liberal and revolutionary, for he does not believe that in history a perfect and frustrationless society will be reached. Yet in historical retrospect, the conservative may claim that some connection between political promise and political fact does exist. As the conservative spirit witnesses its eternal rebirth from the disintegration of the revolution, it may observe with some dispassionateness the fusion of old enemies, now reformed or more instructed in political prudence; it may recognize the force of frustration generated in periods of war, external stress, and the changes of political power; it may consider as a curable evil the psychological fatigue that may immunize the mass of men to the call of any ideal save that of public order; it may safely rationalize the partial reform and consider it a worthy achievement, even though it may fall short of the ideal of justice; but more important still, it may witness with appreciation the resurgence of old values that in other periods have animated constructively the course of history.

Thus, in the period of transition and equilibrium between a resurgent conservatism and a disintegrating liberalism, the ancient polarities of human conflict can be seen again, and with this insight we perceive some of the methods for dealing with them that have been tried in other, and even in remote, periods of history. In contemporary democracy and despotism there are few new elements, nor are there any new values, but it does not mean that the conflict is any the less severe because of it. Of the longstanding polarities of politics, we may mention the conflict between order or authority and liberty, between the ideal of human justice and perennial adjustment to political distortion, between the rich who would defend their position and the poor who demand security and some of the wealth of spirit that is possible to men, between the affirmation of morality and the acceptance of the opportune, and finally between a government of law and the harsh return of political tyranny.

The contemporary right is fluid. It is clearly in a period of transition in which political leaders struggle with the issues of social reconstruction that have followed nearly half a century of war and tension in foreign relations. Our problem is, in part, to state what of value has been left over from the historical conservatism that emerged in Europe after the Napoleonic wars, and to what extent present-day conservatism is a search for ideological and doctrinal bases of continuity in social development. The breakdown of the historic agreement of the democratic West has made inapplicable much of the defense of gradualism, and in its stead it has been essential to recognize that the spirit of conservatism must live through basic notions of public order and through rapid changes or reforms that will preserve these essential ideas.

Among the expressions, then, of contemporary conservatism that has most common ground with its former enemies is a system of foreign policy seeking to check the advance of communism. Foreign affairs is thus the height of politics in the contemporary world. Against his will, the conservative has been driven almost to an either-or position that ill suits his nature. The risk of war and the possible destruction of Western society makes primary much that has been secondary in the former conflicts between liberals and conservatives. Yet the shift of interest from domestic to foreign issues is not the whole story. Even here the issue of the condition of the masses is recognized by all political groups as central in the struggle against the continuous efforts of totalitarianism to get control of the machinery of the Western state system.

Under these conditions it is hardly worth mentioning the forms of conservatism that today have little relevance to the struggles of politics. Just as the revolutionary ideologies of a generation or two ago have been pushed aside and have little connection with present-day politics, so have the older forms of conservatism become the possession of small and peripheral groups of conservatives who have no share in the power of the modern state. Monarchic and aristocratic conservatism today in Europe is a small and curious remnant of another day, for the institutions they would defend have in fact no contribution to make to a new order of political stabilities. An earlier and aristocratic landed system is falling before the claims of the national state for greater agricultural production and the demand for better conditions of life for agricultural workers. In the latter instance, the conservative program characteristically stands for individual ownership of property as a support for the family, while the conservatism of the landlord is losing both its appeal and its ability in Europe to defend itself.

The question of the extension of the suffrage has been in principle settled, since everywhere it has been extended. Even the liberals of predominantly Catholic societies agree that women may be given the right to vote, while the conservatives, in Latin America for example, have surrendered their defense of both literacy and property tests. Perón, like Gallegos, has extended the right to vote to women. If the formal remains of aristocracy have no political force, as in England or Italy, neither a resurgent political conservatism nor a disintegrating liberalism has dealt adequately with bureaucratic and military abuses. The civil service and the military stand, indeed, at the core of the modern state and they hold the positions from which any new social policies must be executed. And while the franchise has become all but a universally granted privilege, the frustration of honest elections has made all that leads up to and follows free elections of fundamental concern. In truth, the defense of free elections, with all they imply both before and after, has become one of the primary grounds of consensus between conservatives and liberals as they both seek to turn back the tide of revolutionary tyranny.

The central issues that any political movement must face today are clear. What are the elements of sound public order? What is the place of constitutional government in politics? Is not the defense of political democracy the only basis of order, continuity, and freedom? What are the proposals that must be accepted in the reconstruction of the social and economic order? What can a democrat do about the intransigent opposition that is unwilling to let free elections follow each other in orderly succession? The classification of conservatism, like that of other movements, arises from its evolution. But it would seem that the primary characteristic of political conservatism at the present time is its defense of traditional democracy, seeking through foreign policy and world organization to defend it on an international scale. Here is the deeper perspective of public order, but in a secondary sense it recognizes that such social reforms must be enacted that the claim to personality of all members of the state will be recognized in moral, social, and economic matters. The contemporary right is a fluid conservatism that seeks the defense of older and primary values through an acceleration of change in political habits and economic arrangements.

41

V

The contemporary conservative defender of democracy faces an issue that was hardly conceived of when the modern techniques for expressing the sovereignty of the people were shaped. For, a century ago, it was assumed that when the people were given power they would use it, and use it to the limit. But when the tyranny of the masses, or the majority, did not materialize, the first interpretation was that the masses were conservative—indeed, far more conservative than the educated classes. Henry S. Maine framed his argument against democracy in these terms: aristocrats constitute a progressive force, a creative minority, against the inertia and unprogressiveness of the masses. The tyranny of the majority meant, in effect, the destruction of the very possibility of progressive change. And with Bagehot the thick crust of custom was a work of the uncreative masses; it had to be broken by the processes of change supported by the more flexible and the educated elite. Today, when we see large numbers of ordinary people following the false prophets of tyrannical doctrine, we may be impressed with Toynbee's conclusion that the creative minority and uncreative and imitative masses form the fundamental division in a society.

While Sir Henry Maine could see that wirepullers and manipulators dominate democracy, he did not reach a theory of the process of politics in which oligarchy and organization leave the members of the majority with hardly any political power, but which, at the same time, puts a new and stunning meaning into the idea of the tyranny of the majority. In other words, he could not explain why the masses did not reach out individually and seize government in actual democratic politics. Or one might cite Lord Bryce who saw in the bosses and machines of American politics a temporary aberration that soon would be overcome by the more simple remedies available to the democratic state. But before the rise of the totalitarian state, masquerading under the forms of democracy, the theory of political process was beginning to be formulated. However, we can hardly find here an imagination bold enough to conceive of the system of manipulative techniques that has been used by the authoritarian state, and which is clearly behind the façade of so-called democratic defense to be found in fascism and communism.

In the evolution of conservative theory, by which it made its adjustment to democracy, as earlier fears proved to be ungrounded, it is clear there was little perception of the perverse possibilities of the democratic process. It could not be imagined that the whole system by which the masses were given power was to become the backbone of the system of modern political slavery. Yet such a paradoxical result has produced the current issue of the nature of free elections, and it has altered profoundly the conservative appreciation of democracy.

We have thus in our time a renewed perception of the issue of constitutional government. With the advent of democracy, the rule of law could no longer be the code of oligarchic or aristocratic groups of holders of social and political power. Constitutional government, in the present crisis in the West, must be reformulated and retaught in the light of the ideal sovereignty of the people. Yet that light must be refracted or diffused through the realistic process under which sovereignty is exercised. Clearly, the rule of law embodied in a constitution serves various purposes. It has one coloration if its purpose is to check executive, legislative, or judicial excesses; it has another if it is a check against the tyranny of the majority; it has another if the issue is the control of party oligarchy and the privileges of democratic placement; and, finally, it has another if the issue is seen, not as excesisve power in the executive or any other organ of government, not as too great a seizure of power by the ordinary citizen, not as the interposition of irresponsible party conclaves, but as the existence of a permanent, inescapable, and only partially controllable process of politics. Here the rule of law is not so much the creation of constitutional norm as it is the creation of conditions under which the people in the mass exercise to some degree the potential of their power. In the extreme, the democratic problem, through constitutional government, is to create a condition under which the tyranny of the majority is conceivable, or in which the process of political control is limited in its impact on the people themselves.

The conservative problem in the current international defense of constitutional democracy is much like the older, radical statement of it. It is a restoration of government, in measure at least, to the people. But it is a restoration that will remove the political process from the control of revolutionary and unscrupulous elites who have spoken with strident prophecy in the name of the common man. In warring against the revolutionary tide of the present, much as

a conservative Europe sought with success to contain the
French Revolution, the contemporary right seeks to preserve
or to re-establish free elections. But such an election implies
honorable opposition, not an intransigent fury of opposi-
tional epithet; it implies the competition of ideas, not the
governmental support of one official orthodoxy; it implies
a constitutional process, orderly and precise, in the conduct
of elections, and not the faking of election returns; and
finally it implies that the state shall be governed by the
results of elections, and that another free election will follow
at the appointed time. It implies, above all, that political
discussion and the selection of public policy and personnel
are not phases or techniques in civil war, for civil war in
effect falsifies the whole democratic process.

Such a conservative defense of the democratic tradition
is surely a far cry from the conservative reaction to the first
stirrings of democracy in the modern world. But it is not
so far as one might think, for one of the central arguments
of nineteenth-century conservatism was the defense of intermediate social groups in the state against the naked principle of the French Revolution that there should be no
groupings or associations between the individual and the
government. Alexis de Tocqueville was keenly aware of
this problem, for the breakdown of intermediate powers and
social groups and the rise of a stark individualism in politics
were themselves the precursors of the Revolution in France.
The defense of the voluntary association, of the right of the
corporate body, whether religious or otherwise, to exist and
share in state power, the function of the intermediate and
local political grouping, was in origin a criticism of the

theory of democracy. While the theory of the French Revolution was impractical and utopian, and new democratic groupings took shape, it remained to our time for the totalitarian state to deny, through the modern tyranny, the right of the citizen to form the natural groups of society. Thus, I think we can say that implicit in the doctrine of the free election is a defense of free groupings, of intermediate powers, and voluntary associations that, through the total process of democracy, can share in the power of the state. One might even say there is a line of continuity between the defense of the function of the historic aristocracy and the restatement of the nature of a free election. For the process of a free election focuses for the moment the whole body of political rights that free citizens may have.

This argument is clearly in line with the principles of balance and moderation in the conduct of the state; it reflects the most ancient and the highest ideals of political prudence. It avoids the common abyss of both unchecked political cynicism and a schizophrenic utopianism, for both are dangerous to the existence of democracy. The intransigent opposition, that destroys finally the rule of law, nurtures the people with ideologies that in our time combine both cynicism in technique and utopianism in end, and which alternate with erratic violence between the two. Such a conservatism would check the power of unbalanced propaganda and the use of modern techniques of revolution and dictatorial control. Such a conservatism, struggling today through the channels of foreign policy, may give the ideals of the Western moral order a chance to be expressed again through political gradualism, by giving some reality to the sovereignty of the people, and by some check to the manipulators of the revolutionary party oligarchy. Under these conditions a state must pay some attention to what its citizens may desire, or what their long-run and permanently formulated opinions may demand.

VI

After the Napoleonic wars there was a new perception of social and political issues, in which extreme positions jarred each other in the conflicts of succeeding generations. But that conflict made it clear that for society to exist there must be public order and an effective production of the goods by which society lives. Much of conservatism in a time of crisis like the present is devoted to fostering these elemental aspects of society. The modern liberal who has had enough of revolution from the East may understand this better at this time than after the Napoleonic period. Yet the conservative today knows that the causes of crisis run deep, and that profound changes in economic arrangements must be attained if the critical time is to be surmounted. In this the liberal will give support, knowing as the conservative does, that the restoration of the rule of law, in the form of constitutional democracy, is the only context in which freedom and useful reform are possible.

Thus it is only under parliamentary or democratic institutions that the historic forces for order, freedom, and beneficial reform may bring together in some community of agreement the political antagonists of another time. But if this is a time of reform and change, the conservative will say that the primary ideas of conservative reform do not coincide in principle with the liberal, as Sir Richard Austen Butler has insisted. The basis of compromise cannot be found entirely in philosophy, for the materialism and scientism of the liberal is hardly reconcilable with the theistic philosophy of social Christianity. Yet agreement and common purpose can be found, not only in the support of constitutional government, but in the effort to reach reforms that will extend the benefits of technological society to the ordinary citizen. The conservative, like the Christian democrat in Italy, cannot accept the principle of the class struggle, and he will not desert the validity of the concept of private property functioning on behalf of the family. But both liberals and conservatives may agree that the land tenure system must be reformed, and that the abuses of industrial society must be constantly in the minds of those who frame legislation. The liberal, long anti-clerical in his perceptions, may find that social Christianity will support much of his program for reform.

Moreover, both conservatives and liberals must struggle against some of those who, in the name of friendship, carry principles to extreme and impractical application. Any reaction is, indeed, simply an excess, a distortion of principle. Stalin's state socialism has mocked and demoralized the democratic socialist and liberal movement all over the world; and the nationalistic extremism of Franco, Perón, and others compromises the conservatism of Christian democracy. Whatever else it may be, conservatism, as a spirit in politics, is an eternal demand for political moderation, and for an evolving continuity, in which reform may be attained without the psychiatric fury of nationalism or the intransigent hatred of revolutionary Marxism.

48

THE AMERICAN CONSERVATIVE TRADITION

I

IN 1841 Ralph Waldo Emerson observed, with his usual ministerial good will, that the party of conservatism and the party of innovation "have disputed the possession of the world ever since it was made." The conflict, he said, is deeply seated in the human constitution, which is no doubt true. But Emerson's conservatives and innovators correspond to little that might be found in either history or space, for the conservative to him was simply a defender of the *status quo,* and conservatism is "the pause on the last movement." Conservatism was all memory. While the conservative and innovator each made a good half, each made an impossible whole. And further, he argued, sensing the weakness of his political poetry, the very posibility of reform grows out of universal and necessary history; conservatism gives innovation its chance.

Conservatives do not regard themselves as merely a half of the social picture. The conservative spirit, they would argue, is a totality and a wiry answer to the issues of the world, but as in all other poltical debates it is difficult to cross or recross the line of understanding running between positions. Thus Henri-Frédéric Amiel expressed, from the standpoint of a vigorous Calvinism, the aspiration to reality in conservatism. "Let us not, then," he said on November 7, 1862, "condemn prejudice so long as we have nothing but doubt to put in its place, or laugh at those we should be incapable of consoling." He saw clearly the issue presented by the radical and the revolutionary of the last century. Especially on the morrow of the Paris Commune was the issue like the page of an illuminated book. The socialism of the workers, he observed on June 21, 1871, in his *Journal Intime,* has been put down ineffectually in Paris. Now the socialists begin to celebrate their victory against country, historical memory, property, and religion. The International (the first one, that is) is but the pioneer of a conquering Russian nihilism which will be the common grave of old races. Amiel saw that a succession of opposing follies gives the impression of change and improvement, but he argued to himself that the error of the Demos is only equaled by its presumption. There is a fiction that the majority has reason on its side, he thought, but the ignorant do not have to train themselves to act. In consequence, humanity takes the longest road to an end. "The mode of progress in the moral world," he said, "seems an abuse of the patience of God."

Like the antiquaries of the sixteenth and seventeenth centuries, we must search anew in our time for the significance of corporate or national experience. Those who do this are, in effect, conservative in spirit, and, as then, one of the defenses of current policy is to argue its harmony with

continuities from the past. The conservative spirit, in the
United States as elsewhere, has insisted that the most soundly
based progress arises from moral reform, while the revolutionary (the natural opponent of the conservative) looks to
a changing structure to bring it about. Yet as revolutionary
thought changes with the historical eddy, so does conservatism, and there is quite inevitably a periodical revision of
the conservative spirit in spite of its continuities. From an
emphasis on spirit and moral responsibility rather than
structure, conservative attention falls upon political art, or
political prudence, to effect an adjustment to the times.
While adherence to tradition signifies the endurance of
moral responsibility, the inevitable and necessary political
art indicates a sharp sensibility to experience and the effort
to make the state the fulfillment of the nation's will.

Conservative spirit in America is thus never simply a
defense of things as they are, for at the height it seeks to
blend the fading past and the emerging future into an
imaginative present. What it can never do is to relieve
men of their responsibility in the vast context of experience. By contrast, if we would summarize the revolutionary
urge of our day in the West, we would say that man is the
victim and not the life force of a social system. Here is the
false doctrine that destroys both tradition and a capable
political art. Because man is the victim, he must submerge
himself in the mass to overthrow continuity. Institutions
must be destroyed in the name of humanitarian impulse.
But the time comes when the submerged man knows that he
has no responsibility, and true humanitarianism is destroyed
through murder and tyranny. Men are no longer brothers,

America and it has made our history. Like Ranke, our conservatives would agree that honest conservative politics is to hold the essence of the past. Like German or English conservatism of the nineteenth century, our conservatism has been in part a reaction against the revolution we have not loved, but it has also been, on the positive side, an attempt to define and defend the permanent interests and institutions of a good society. That will always be one of the functions of conservative thought, quite regardless of what other burdens the changing age may impose. Conservatism does not scorn the ideal, for it defines it and tries to show how effort for its realization may be effective or destructive. With nations as with men, we might say with H. A. L. Fisher, "the colder wisdom of the age uses and refines the sanguine enthusiasm of youth."

Moreover, in this age of war, of great and unhappy cities, and of undreamed of industrialization, the conservative function is in no little part to remind the urban capitalist and worker that there are permanent interests in the state that are continuous with a precapitalist era. This is to say, there is a tradition behind any successful society; but Americans sometimes need to be reminded that religion is a social interest, that culture and the progress of all of the arts cannot be forgotten, that society must have a landed interest as well as a factory system, that political structures must be responsible if they would grow into the affection of the people, and that the international position of the state requires the constant labor of statesmanship. But all, including conservatives when they drift toward reaction, which is simply an excess or a defect in principle, need to be reminded that the exis-

tence of the community means that there are common interests and duties, and that it is the duty of philosophy, as well
as government, to secure their recognition, and to prevent
the destruction of the traditions of a common life.

In a discussion of conservatism we may speak of the party
of order as against the party of progress, we may contrast
stability with change, experience may be set against experiment, historical continuity against utopian breaks with the
past, an orderly and dynamic system of inequality against
revolutionary egalitarianism, the defense of tradition against
government by propaganda, of moral duty against the revolutionary loss of human dignity, and the defense of liberty
and property against modern political totalitarianism.

Most American conservatives have at least paid lip-service
to these ideas. American conservatives participated in a revolution in part because the policy of the British government
violated the traditional conception Americans held of the
British Constitution. American conservatives established order under the new American Constitution, and since then
have been its most consistent defenders. Perhaps the first
major succeeding task was the establishment of the middle
and commercial classes firmly in our society through a series
of distinctly conservative, i.e., Hamiltonian, reforms. Conservative spirit defended the Union against the southern bid
for independence, though many reconstruction policies must
be regarded as aberrations. Broadly, American conservatism
has been Protestant, and the defense of a Protestant culture
may still be regarded as a conservative drive. Yet with the
changes in our cultural tradition this era must be all but
concluded. As in England, the defense of agriculture and the

principle of land ownership has been a part of American conservatism, as well as the security of national territory. A central question, however, is the evaluation of the defense of capitalistic enterprise in the scheme of American conservatism. The enormous growth of American industrialism after Appomattox must, it would seem, be regarded as a transitional phase of our development. In harmony with urban-minded liberalism, American capitalistic conservatism forgot that national achievement must be based on a balance of the permanent social forces in society. The re-evaluation of industrialism is clearly one of the central issues of modern thought.

II

In the short time at my disposal, little can be said of many developments in American conservative thought. However, I hope I can group some of the major trends together and generalize, perhaps rather sketchily, about their development. Some of the major statements from men in public life should be considered, as well as the political structures they have favored. Religion and its political tradition in the United States, as well as the humanitarian impulse, should be given some consideration. What the economists have said is worthy of our attention, and even what we might call popular success literature deserves treatment in the story of the development of our conservative mind. Finally, some brief attention must be given to certain writers who can, perhaps, best be classified simply as intellectuals.

When we speak of public life and the men in it we are considering the ruling order in our society. While we must bear in mind that power as a descriptive fact is ideologically neutral, we must remember that the purposes of power, and the organization of power, can reflect the ends for which society is acknowledged to exist. The messages and papers of presidents of the United States constitute a great mine of conservative statement, from which we might draw the rest of our discussion. But I would say that one of the easiest places to start is with the authors of *The Federalist.* In my opinion, this series of papers ranks with the writings of Burke in the creation of the modern conservative spirit in politics. While it was written before the French Revolution was under way, it could have been written later. It could have been written in more detached circumstances and after the theoretical achievements of the Revolution in France, since its attitude toward politics is contrary to the idea of a doctrinaire and unlimited humanitarianism.

But some might say that Madison, Hamilton, and Jay, the authors of the immortal *Federalist,* were themselves revolutionists, and that the men they opposed were the Tories, the real conservatives of that day. The same, I suppose, might be said of Washington and John Adams, or any other of the generation who formed the Constitution of the United States, and who provided leadership for the emergent Federalist party. But I think we may insist that there is a continuity of ideas from the revolution through the formation of the Constitution. In this continuity we find a constant insistence on the consent of the governed, on the rights of man, and on a structure of government that might establish the protection of life, liberty, and property, the rights of man we most commonly accept. Let us remember there is no mystery in the conservative as a revolutionary, for it has often been so. It is so today among those who would preserve the continuity of Western society against the encroachment of Slavic ideology.

In our origins there is, however, this difference. While Burke appealed both to the established principles of the British Constitution and to the principles of sound government, our leaders could appeal only to the principles of society on which they believed a just system might exist. North American and Latin-American conservatives have this in common: they both helped fight a revolution for the principles they believed to be correct, and neither could appeal directly to the legal continuity of the state as Burke did. On basic social principles, perhaps the American loyalist had much in common with the leaders of the American Revolution, such as George Washington, but on the defense of the actual British government there was the widest disparity. After the Revolution was won, the American conservative could continue, as before, the defense of the principles of constitutional liberty that he believed had been secured in some measure in British government. It was the liberals, such as Jefferson, who turned for inspiration to the newly arising French systems of thought, who continued to regard British institutions with a jaundiced eye.

While *The Federalist* was a defense of the Constitution as it was drawn in 1787, while it is a defense of the rights of man and the consent of the governed, and while it regards balance and mixture as proper elements in a just government, it was not enthusiastic about unlimited political participation, and it defended the rights of the judiciary with energy. It believed in a strong executive and the strengthening of the national Union. One might say, I think, that the conservative view of human nature as a mixture of the rational and irrational finds full expression in its pages. The writers in *The Federalist* were interested, it seems to me, in the preconditions of majority rule. The precondition they insisted on was intelligence in government; perhaps we might say even, as was said during the nineteenth century in France particularly, that they believed in the sovereignty of intelligence or of justice. They believed, I think, that a just government was the only legitimate one, and that the consent of the governed became legitimate to the extent that intelligence and justice were expressed through the people. The Constitution of the United States, viewed in this light, becomes a great effort to assure the preservation of the social principles that are a part of intelligence and justice, and it is, therefore, an effort to secure on principle the existence of legitimacy in government.

As the liberal thinkers moved more and more toward a purified majority rule, the conservative mind in public life continued to insist that majority rule had its preconditions. That mind insisted that men had other rights than to be included in a majority. The judiciary, arising from the original consent of the people to the Constitution, was the instrument by which the rights of men, especially to their property, were to be protected. The critics of national power, and those who sought an unrestricted majority, one that might be the final interpreter of the bill of rights, were therefore together in their criticism of the judiciary. One might here balance the ideas of Jefferson and Jackson against the thought of both John Adams and John Quincy Adams.

In the period after the Confederate War, when the great movement toward economic and political reform got underway, we can observe a classic renewal of the old battle. Broadly, the second era of democratic reform sought to take out of both state and national constitutions any devices that filtered the wishes of the majority. Since manhood suffrage had long since arrived, and with it the realization that the people were not so radical as the old Federalists had feared, the new struggle centered on the principles of indirect election and establishment of intermediate representative bodies, such as party conventions. I do not think that we need to criticize at all the idea that a political party should be responsible, that is, that it should perform its functions. But it should be remembered that in the thought of a man like Robert M. LaFollette, Sr., there was a strong doctrinaire element. The people were wise, he said, and they were also progressive. But give them the chance and the program of the Progressive movement would be enacted into law. Therefore, it was said, let us have the direct primary, let us have presidential primaries, let us control the national party convention, let us elect senators directly, let us elect the presidents more directly, let us have the initiative, referendum and recall, and, finally, give the people a chance, through their congressional representatives, to override a decision of the Supreme Court. In other words, let us remove entirely from our constitutional system any remnants of indirect election, that nineteenth century principle to which conserva tives adhered and which de Tocqueville saw so clearly as an element in the American political structure.

The conservative response was varied. Men like Nicholas Murray Butler, William Howard Taft, and Elihu Root, most important of all, defended the traditional system of the sovereignty of the people. I think Elihu Root should be studied more carefully than any of the others, for Root was at the same time a vigorous enemy of corruption in government. But he believed that it was unwise to amend too freely the Constitution, and he would preserve the Senate as a body representative of the states, chosen by the legislatures of the states. And he was unimpressed with the doctrine that the initiative and referendum would create a totally new expression of the sovereignty of the people. In the event, we now see that both the Progressive defenders of the new devices, and the conservatives who feared they would destroy representative government, were wrong. The Progressives were wrong, since the political party retained much of the power it had before the introduction of the direct primary, and the initiative and referendum might be used by special interests as readily as by the sovereign people as a whole. The conservatives were wrong because their fears were exaggerated, just as the older Federalists had been too fearful of a Jacobin democracy. They had thought that giving the people the right to vote would mean they would vote. Indeed, during the nineteenth-century battle over the extension of democracy, all leaders, progressives or otherwise, were under the delusion that if the people had the power to run the government they would exercise their power to the full. These leaders showed no political realism, for they did not realize that the power of the leadership of the few rests on political psychology and not on structure of the government.

In concluding this section, I might observe that extreme movements, such as Populism, or formal ideological parties, from the rise of socialism in America to the fall of Henry Agard Wallace, have seldom had much success. The ancient common law idea, that monopolies are a bad influence on the body politic, has generally been used to make attempts to correct the abuses of the economic system. The denunciation of monopoly has been for a long time a good plank in anybody's political platform. Property is only moderately under attack through a system of taxation that in some respects is not far from confiscation. But we are not now concerned with restricting the right to vote. We are concerned, however, with the falsification of the right to vote through the organizing force of pressure groups. And today, as in the past, we are concerned with the preconditions of majority rule so that the public interest, that is, the standards of behavior suitable for a whole society, will not be sacrificed through the indifference of the many.

III

If we turn to another phase of this question, we can easily remember that the American dream of democracy, the vision of a free republic carrying the mission of freedom to all, has been a deeply religious idea. Protestantism in the United States has been both profoundly humanitarian and bluntly provincial. But I think one can say that one feature of the long predominance of Protestantism in American religious and political thought has been the development of an

American and peculiarly Protestant philosophy of history. It has been assumed that America will always be Protestant, whereas now we have a multireligious tradition in a society that is largely secular and materialistic in outlook, perhaps even substantially pagan.

Nineteenth-century Protestantism tended to be, on the whole, optimistic and humanitarian. It gradually ceased to fear the radicalism of Europe, especially that of France, and the history of the United States from generation to generation seemed to document effectively the providence of God. In its sharper moods, it denounced the growth of the Catholic faith in the United States, and it looked with disturbance on the religious ideas of Europeans who did not share in its tradition. But until recent times it was felt that the immigrant would, after his Americanization, fit into the older American Protestant tradition, which was, indeed, identified with liberty, republicanism, and humanitarian democracy. Timothy Dwight fought against the encroachment of French infidelity in American deistic liberalism, and his successor at Yale, James McCosh, defended the moral foundations of Protestant life against Boston and Harvard Unitarianism and the secularist implications of science. His concept of divine government included a healthy skepticism as to the influence of the masses in government. With the voice of the Calvinist he declared roundly in 1874 that "in the systems of the Communists there can be no provision made for guiding and controlling such a conglomerate of sentiments and lusts." While social miseries are necessary to prevent greater evils, he concluded that God intended a restoration of man through progress under his concept of

Protestant history. Nor should we omit Mark Hopkins from those who expounded the American and Protestant philosophy of history. Henry Ward Beecher, and Lyman Abbott, his successor in Brooklyn, continued the tradition, but with a more optimistic and humanitarian type of thought. Protestantism, offered by the Anglo-Saxon race, carried with it the principle of civilization.

We must not forget, in dealing with such men, that they were concerned, like Lincoln, about defending the national interest. They did not believe that humanitarianism could be limited when it was combined with American liberty. In a sense, they believed that we had reached the height of the ages, very much as Hegel, another great exponent of the Protestant theory of history, believed that he also had witnessed in Protestant Prussia the climax of all ages. Whatever we may say of it, it was a vast attempt to defend the American tradition in a world that did not accept it. And if we compare the world, since the Russian Revolution, with the vision they defended, it is clear what choice would be made. Today our problem is not the defense of Protestantism with its philosophy of history, but the defense of religion at all. Against a common enemy America no doubt needs a vigorous Protestantism along with an energetic Catholicism, and a forceful Judaism in order to defend the national interest and to keep alive the humanitarian tradition that belongs to the religious traditions of the West.

IV

Let us now turn to the economists. Too much attention, I think, has been given to the academic economists, from

Adam Smith to the present, in the statement of the principles of conservatism. Were not the economists the children of their age? Did they not rationalize the Industrial Revolution? And in measure is not that their function today? One thing is clear, however, and that is that much economic literature during the last two centuries has been a capitalistic protest against what the capitalistic societies were actually including in their public policy. Take free trade as an example. For most of the history of the doctrine it has been a protest against governmental restrictions on trade. William Graham Sumner was a dreamer, a man with a vision of a laissez-faire society that had never existed, and probably never will. E. L. Godkin, the nineteenth-century editor of the *Nation* was, like Sumner, a protester against the lack of free trade and laissez-faire in the period that we now, in retrospect, usually assume to have been dominated by that idea. Godkin and Sumner, like the economists in general, observed the government in the business of promotion and subsidy, they saw it enact protective tariffs, and they saw government, even in the grim days following the Civil War, taxing the honest man in order to give benefits to the shiftless and the incompetent. Moreover, economic liberalism generally believed that if free competition, the free market, were ever established throughout the world, a new and mighty period of prosperity would come to all.

Capitalism as a practical political system is, therefore, widely different in our history from the capitalism of economic theory and the academic chair. Economic theory, in this sense, is, I think, one of the utopias of the modern world. It has probably been more a theory of how society might be organized economically than it has been a description of what economic and political society actually was. The day-to-day exponents of modern industrialism have been generally in favor of having the government on their side.

However utopian economic theory may have been, in a larger sense the economists have tried to explain the vast accumulation of capital, the rise in wages, the most remarkable production of consumer goods in the history of the world, and the general progress of the United States and other industrial powers toward the unique position they hold or have held in the course of human history. While Francis A. Walker once said that it was not the province of the economist to justify the existing order of things or to establish the morality of laws relating to property, he could not in fact maintain such a detached position. As other economists, he was forced to consider those public policies that would most enable a society to produce and distribute wealth. If legislation fosters competition, it is good; otherwise the intrusion of special demands into legislation is injurious to the common good. And in the late nineteenth century the criticism of socialism became increasingly important in the literature of American economics. We might spend our time also on a consideration of the economic criticism of various and sundry popular economic panaceas, such as easy money, or the single tax.

But other matters should merit our attention. The American economists have in general defended the right of private property in capital goods, and the utility of a free enterprise system in the accumulation of the capital necessary for high productivity. The economists have believed that capital accumulation, plus a steady march in technological improvement, plus the reluctance of government to adopt socializing schemes, has explained the standard of living and the war-like capacity of the United States. And I think the scholarly labors of John Bates Clark in the theory of economic competition should not be omitted from this discussion.

As you are aware, the idea of competition is one of the most controversial in economic literature. Against competition, as the law of the jungle, the revolutionary mind has set up the ideal of coöperation and socialization, and all of the catalogued evils of human nature have been attached to the profit motive and the competitive principle. One must note, however, that the picture of competition given by the critical mind has little resemblance to the theory of competition given by those who defend it as a principle of civilized economic society. Clark's theme was that we must rescue competition from its perversions, because the civilized competitive principle is essential in the emergence of the capacity to produce. We must strive, he said, to reach a golden mean between letting the state do nothing and asking it to do everything. More real competition, he said, means more production.

The preservation of competition, as a system of moral and civilized rules of the game, meant to Clark, however, significant government intervention in economic life. He favored anti-trust legislation, tariff reform, the conservation of natural resources and laws that would protect private initiative against the encroachments of monopoly. All honest capitalists are allied with honest labor, he said, for they both, along with the great middle class, are interested mainly in the same reforms. And, to gain these ends, it is essential to improve the control by the people over the government. Thus Clark favored the movement toward direct legislation. But beyond this there should be a shorter working day, accompanied by improvements in the efficiency of labor. Workers are entitled to protection against industrial dangers, and Clark favored compensation legislation and the pure food laws. With a lower tariff, a reform in the money and banking system would help mitigate economic crises. We should prevent the waste of natural resources, develop the parcel post, the use of the telephone and telegraph systems, and the transportation systems of our cities. There should be a simplified court procedure and cheaper courts, and small investments should be stimulated and protected, especially through an extension of the ownership of shares in corporate enterprises. But the great evil is monopoly, for only by attacking monopoly can we be sure of increasing competition and thereby the greater use of inventions.

Some of these reforms sound pale enough today, forty years after they were proposed. But what happened was that the economist, such as Simon N. Patten, came to believe in a kind of competitive utopia, one that would insure the future progress of our society. They failed to see, I believe, the complexity of the problem of preserving competition, and they assumed that war would not be the destroying angel it has been during the first half of the twentieth century. The economists did, like Thomas N. Carver, recognize that competition must be preserved by government action, and competition under these conditions could become remote from a savage struggle for survival. It became to some, indeed,

more the expression of Christian justice than the evil characteristic of so much of human behavior. In the large literary
remains of a man like Andrew Carnegie, for example, we
find the competitive principle identified with the humanitarian idea of life and the assurance that economic competition would work for the peace of the world.

Yet so far as I know no system of social theory, save the
religious, takes adequate account of the tragedy of human
life. In this, American humanitarianism, if I mistake not,
has often been at fault, for it has thought the tragedy of life
to be an aberration that republican industrialism can surely
cure. A social system creates its structure of power with the
impersonality and fixity of skyscrapers. The revolution
draws its strength from the fatuous promise that it will meet
the issue of tragedy in life. And in the result, it does not fulfill
its promises; it has to fill the void with the promise of another day that will be better. Ordinarily, conservatism makes
no such promises; it does not assure its followers that as far
as material things are concerned there will be an abundance
for all. It does, however, construct the hope that progress can
be made, and the principles of economic progress are one of
the lasting elements in American conservative theory.

V

We turn now to another facet of this subject. Part of the
defense of the American system has been the promise of opportunity to the willing hand, and the assurance that ordinary men can and do share in our wealth more than in other
lands. As long as there was free trade in ideas in Europe, no
one could contest the success of the ordinary man in Amer-

ica. But with the development of the modern art of propaganda, and the isolation of whole peoples from accurate information about the United States, another picture of America as a land ground down by poverty and misery is earnestly and successfully propagated behind the Iron Curtain. In spite of this powerful censorship and the inevitable distortions it produces, it is still the dream of millions of displaced and frustrated Europeans to come to the United States to share its wide political and economic liberty. I for one would not want to discount too much the power of this popular appreciation of what the American political and economic system is like.

But it is true, on the other hand, that our popular conservatism has been propagated by a singularly inane type of success literature. Success is a common thing in these United States, and each week brings over the horizon another unknown who has risen to greatness in economic or business activity, political effort, literary creativeness, scientific discovery, or new technological inventiveness. Yesterday we said that this is the meaning of our American life; today we take it as a matter of course. Yesterday we said the process justified itself as in the philanthropic leadership of a man like Andrew Carnegie, but today we tend to count the cost in the number of contestants for high honor who fall by the way and need the helping, but hardly brotherly, hand of a social security system. I do not think I need to add that the revolutionary mind teaches with enthusiasm that all success, save that in the proletarian cause, is illegitimate, and that it is based on the destruction of the chances of a fellow-citizen. Certainly, one thing the conservative spirit in America seeks to do today is to justify the right of a man to be successful, and that the individual who shows some excellent capacity should be honored by his fellow citizens. Such achievement must be recognized, the conservative would say, in building a fortune as well as in becoming a prominent citizen of the star-studded world of filmdom.

The names of Horatio Alger, Elbert Hubbard, Orison S. Marden, William H. Thayer, Russell H. Conwell, and others were once common household symbols in the United States. *Acres of Diamonds* and *A Message to Garcia* once covered the land, and the message to Garcia was no doubt a message to the world for a time. Those who lectured and wrote on success were among the last to enjoy what Vernon Louis Parrington called "the great barbecue," or perhaps they were the Epigoni of the Gilded Age. Yet these prophets of individual success based on character have passed, and those who have followed them feed upon the fragments of a once significant tradition. These successors are the exponents of a corrupted, perverted, and debased psychology; they are the advocates of physical culture and the body beautiful; they revel in and reveal the intimate details of the aristocracy of Hollywood; and they esoterically preach the exoteric in religion.

The titles of another day reveal the story. If we would, we might read today *From Log-Cabin to the White House, The Pioneer Boy and How He Became President, Onward to Fame and Fortune, Bound to Rise, Joe's Luck, Pushing to the Front, He Can Who Thinks He Can, Do It to a Finish,* and scores of others, including the strangely prejudiced *Little Journeys* of Elbert Hubbard, who was an Illinois farm boy who became the first great soap salesman in our history.

Yet some reservations might be made. American individualism, as taught in the literature of success, did not argue that we could all be rich, but that all of us with an honorable effort might support ourselves and our families, and that we might achieve something worthy of a human life. It taught that there are rewards for virtue in the material world, and that men of Christian character and of sturdy will might attain social security through their own efforts. No conservative will deny the importance of individual character, and in no society are the listless and the irresponsible welcomed. But social philosophy today, whether Christian or otherwise, sees clearly that character alone is not sufficient for the creation of the orderly and moral life. Success literature took its stand upon a single but important factor, that of individual character. Swept away by enthusiasm for the new industrial system, it generalized from the fact that poor farm boys frequently get rich when they go to the big cities. Indeed, it seemed to suggest that this was a characteristic of the big city. It did not see that great success was the reward of the few, whether for virtue or not, and that the many were left behind in the struggle for wealth.

VI

I must say a final word on the intellectual climate of the conservative spirit. As revolutionary and liberal minds have increasingly accepted uncritically the unleashed power of the new welfare state and the new Leviathan, the conservative has been, in the United States as elsewhere, unwilling to believe that either tyranny or bureaucratic collectivism can serve the purposes of order or progress. In the intellectual and moral realm, American conservative thought has re-affirmed the historic foundations of culture, whatever it may have thought of the immediate conditions in America. The greatest of our intellectual conservatives, Paul Elmer More, set out in a search for the standards of civilized men, and in that search it was primarily to the arts that he turned. His turn was particularly to the written word, the great litera-ture of past days that still was great because of its message to the present. Thus the tradition of humane literature, *belle lettres,* the urbane and the cultivated in the personality, the sovereignty of intelligence, and the justice of moral percep-tiveness were the constituent elements of the aristocracy in a democratic society.

Paul Elmer More cited the long supremacy of Homer to show that the laws of taste were the least changeable facts of human nature. Here, too, we have an inescapable type of tra-dition that a conservative society must accept. Neither new-ness nor age can in themselves serve as criteria of truth, but the difference between civilization and barbarism is the maintenance of this continuity of tradition. This conserva-tism is essential to survival and to self-preservation in the field of the arts.

If we seek for the ultimate conflict between the conserva-tive and the revolutionary spirit in politics, we shall find it in our conceptions of human nature. The modern revolu-tionary view has with fair consistency insisted that man is a malleable creature, and that in the end most evil or frustra-tion arises from the force of external institutions and not from the inner qualities of the spirit. On the contrary, the conservative argues that the spirit of men shapes institutions, that the arrangements of society arise from man as he is, and that reform must arise from historically grounded intelligence and imagination. The distrust of human nature that is characteristic of the conservative spirit must, therefore, be combined with the idea of historical imagination. It is only with poetic or religious insight that man under these circumstances is moving progressively forward. It is only with historical imagination, More argued, that future history can result in action that will deal realistically with men as they are and at the same time retain the notion of progress and a closer, but possible, attainment of the American humanitarian ideal.

The revolutionary mind in its direct attack on the conservative offers us a monistic, either-or position. Man is good or he is bad; you are for progress or you are for reaction; you fight either for the angels or the devils; and in politics you are either a friend or a foe, as Carl Schmitt once argued in his defense of the German National Socialist revolution. This dilemma the conservative will not accept, for it is an attack on all dualism, balance, and moderation in intellectual and cultural life.

The political conservative is, like Paul Elmer More, a dualist. Individuals are unique and spiritual; they stand over against society and the state which is natural in structure and administration, and are, therefore, subject to scientific discussion. When the individual is subjected to the scientifically natural, there remains, finally, no defense against the growth of morally unperceptive power. But as life is changing in its conditions, there must always be new appli-